Questions and Answers: Countries

Saudi Arabia

A Question and Answer Book

by Kathleen W. Deady

Consultant:
Christopher S. Rose
Outreach Coordinator, Center for Middle Eastern Studies
University of Texas, Austin
Austin, Texas

Capstone
press

Mankato, Minnesota

Fact Finders is published by Capstone Press,
151 Good Counsel Drive, P.O. Box 669, Mankato, Minnesota 56002.
www.capstonepress.com

Library of Congress Cataloging-in-Publication Data
Deady, Kathleen W.
Saudi Arabia: A question and answer book / by Kathleen W. Deady.
    p. cm.—(Fact finders. Questions and answers. Countries)
    Includes bibliographical references and index.
    ISBN 0-7368-3760-4 (hardcover)
    1. Saudi Arabia—Juvenile literature. I. Title. II. Series.
DS204.25.D43 2005
953.8—dc22   2004011403

Summary: Describes the geography, history, economy, and culture of Saudi Arabia in a
question-and-answer format.

Editorial Credits
Katy Kudela, editor; Kia Adams, set designer; Kate Opseth, book designer; Nancy Steers,
    map illustrator; Wanda Winch, photo researcher; Scott Thoms, photo editor

Photo Credits
Art Directors/TRIP, cover (background), 4, 9, 11, 12, 14–15, 18, 21; Bruce Coleman Inc./
Bill Foley, cover (foreground); Corbis/Reuters/Peter Macdiarmid, 1; Corbis/Tim De Waele,
19; Corbis Sygma/ Jacques Langevin, 13, 27; The Image Works/HAGA/Kazuyoshi
Nomachi, 16–17, 23; The Image Works/HAGA/Peter Sanders, 25; Mary Evans Picture
Library, 7; Photo courtesy of Richard Sutherland, 29 (bill); Photo courtesy of the Worldwide
Bi-Metal Collectors Club/Paul Baker, 29 (coins); Royal Embassy of Saudi Arabia/Saudi
Information Office, 8; StockHaus Ltd., 29 (flag)

Artistic Effects
Corel, 6; Photodisc/Siede Preis, 16

1 2 3 4 5 6 10 09 08 07 06 05

Table of Contents

Features

Where is Saudi Arabia?

Saudi Arabia is in southwest Asia, also called the Middle East. It is about one-fifth the size of the United States.

Many land features stretch across Saudi Arabia's landscape. Mountains rise along the western coast. A **plateau** in the central area slopes down to the Persian Gulf.

Camels live in the hot deserts of Saudi Arabia. ➤

4

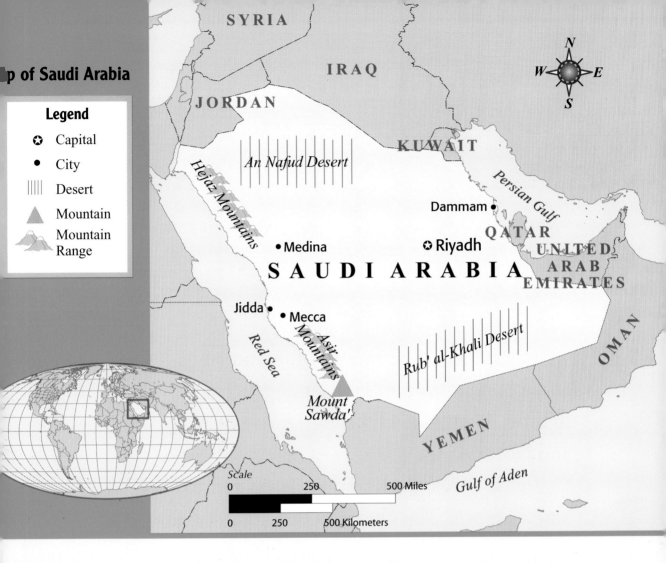

Legend

⊛ Capital
● City
|||| Desert
▲ Mountain
⛰ Mountain Range

SYRIA

IRAQ

JORDAN

KUWAIT

An Nafud Desert

Hejaz Mountains

Dammam ●

Persian Gulf

QATAR

● Medina

⊛ Riyadh

UNITED ARAB EMIRATES

S A U D I   A R A B I A

Jidda ●   ● Mecca

Asir Mountains

Red Sea

Rub' al-Khali Desert

OMAN

Mount Sawda'

YEMEN

Gulf of Aden

Scale
0   250   500 Miles

0   250   500 Kilometers

Large deserts cover the north and south. The Rub' al-Khali Desert in the southeast is the world's largest sand desert.

Saudi Arabia has a very dry climate. Parts of the country may go several years without rain.

5

When did Saudi Arabia become a country?

The Kingdom of Saudi Arabia formed on September 23, 1932. During most of the country's history, it was part of an Islamic empire.

In the 600s, the **prophet** Muhammad became the leader of the Islamic religion. In time, Islam spread through much of Asia and North Africa.

In the 1300s, the Ottoman Turks formed a new empire. The Ottoman Empire grew to include most of Saudi Arabia by the 1600s.

Fact!

Members of the Saud family have ruled Saudi Arabia since 1932.

Abdul Aziz Ibn Saud was Saudi Arabia's first king.

During the next 300 years, people battled over Saudi Arabia's land. In 1902, Abdul Aziz Ibn Saud, an Arab prince, captured the city of Riyadh. He worked to take control of the many groups of people. In 1932, he united them under the Kingdom of Saudi Arabia.

What type of government does Saudi Arabia have?

Saudi Arabia's system of government is a **monarchy**. A king rules the country.

Saudi Arabia has no **constitution**. Since 1993, Saudi Arabia follows the Basic Law. This law sets the rights and duties of the government. The law says the country must follow the laws of the Islamic religion.

The Council of Ministers meets with the king each week. ▶

Fahd Ibn Abdul Aziz is the fifth king of Saudi Arabia. He is a son of Abdul Aziz Ibn Saud.

The king rules with the Council of Ministers. The king chooses members of this group to help him run the country.

Saudi Arabia's kingdom has 14 regions. A leader, called an emir, heads each region. The emirs report to the king.

What kind of housing does Saudi Arabia have?

Most Saudis live in modern houses or apartments in the cities. Many houses have a central courtyard. The courtyard allows a family to gather outdoors in private.

Where do people in Saudi Arabia live?

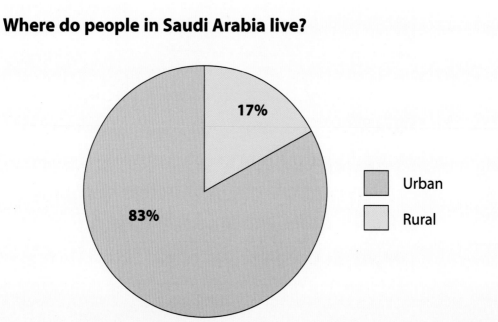

Large apartment buildings are homes for many Saudis.

People outside the cities build their houses from several materials. In central and eastern areas, people use **adobe**. In the west, they use stone and red brick. **Nomads** roam the deserts. They live in tents made from goat or camel skins.

What are Saudi Arabia's forms of transportation?

Saudi Arabia has modern forms of travel. A train connects Dammam to Riyadh. Saudi Arabia also has many airports. People often fly to and from distant cities.

Saudi Arabia's system of paved roads connects large cities. People drive cars. They also ride in taxis or buses.

People use camels to travel through the desert. ➤

Cars crowd the city streets of Saudi Arabia.

Before the 1970s, most people rode camels from place to place. Camels were also the best way to carry heavy loads. In desert areas, some people still use camels. Other people use cars and trucks.

13

What are Saudi Arabia's major industries?

Saudi Arabia's main industry is oil. Saudi Arabia has the largest reserves of **petroleum**, or crude oil, in the world. People use petroleum to make gasoline, heating oil, and other products.

Since the end of World War II (1939–1945), oil has brought great wealth to the Saudi kingdom. Today, Saudi Arabia is the top seller of oil to other countries.

What does Saudi Arabia import and export?	
Imports	*Exports*
chemicals	manufactured goods
food products	petroleum
machinery	petroleum products

*Saudi Arabia sends oil
to other countries.*

Saudi Arabia is building new businesses.
These companies make cement, clothing,
and plastic goods. Saudi Arabia ships some
of these goods to other countries.

What is school like in Saudi Arabia?

Saudi Arabia has three levels of school. Students go to primary school from ages 6 to 12. Students then go to an intermediate school for three years. Secondary school begins at age 15. Students graduate from secondary school at age 18.

Saudi students learn math, history, and science. They also study the Arabic language and the Islamic religion.

Fact!

Saudi Arabia's Islamic law says boys and girls must go to separate schools.

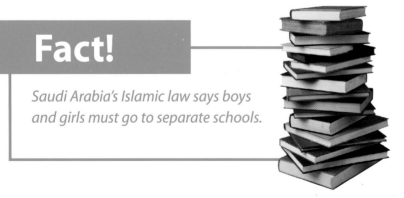

*Saudi students study
the Islamic religion.*

By law, children in Saudi Arabia do not
have to attend school. More Saudi boys go to
school than girls do. Some families believe
education is less important for girls.

What are Saudi Arabia's favorite sports and games?

Soccer is Saudi Arabia's national sport. Many towns have their own fields and soccer clubs.

Hunting sports, such as archery and falconry, are popular. In falconry, people use trained falcons to hunt small animals.

The King's Camel Race is a popular sports event. ▶

In 2002, Saudi Arabia (left) played against the Republic of Ireland in the soccer World Cup finals.

Camel and horse racing are also popular. Each year, people go to the King's Camel Race. During this event, riders race their camels on a racetrack. The racetrack is about 13 miles (21 kilometers) long. As many as 30,000 people come to watch this race.

What are the traditional art forms in Saudi Arabia?

Saudi Arabia has many art forms. People weave carpets. They make crafts from brass, copper, wood, and leather.

Saudis practice the art of handwriting called **calligraphy**. People use calligraphy to decorate pottery and glass. They write lines from the **Koran** on **mosques** and other public buildings.

Fact!

Some Muslims believe that art should not show humans or animals. Instead, artists create flowers and shapes.

Saudi men perform a sword dance called the ardha.

Music and dance are important to the Saudi people. The national dance of Saudi Arabia is the men's sword dance. It is called the *ardha*. Men dance close together while carrying swords. A drummer keeps the beat while a poet sings.

What major holidays do people in Saudi Arabia celebrate?

Saudis observe many religious holidays. During the month of Ramadan, **Muslims** fast. They do not eat or drink from sunrise to sunset. They celebrate the end of this month with Eid al-Fitr. For three days, families enjoy special meals and give each other gifts.

On Eid al-Adha, Muslims remember the prophet Abraham. He was willing to sacrifice his son for God. On this holiday, people kill a lamb and give away the meat.

What other holidays do people in Saudi Arabia celebrate?

Islamic New Year
Jinadriyah National Festival
Laylat al-Mi'raj

Muslims gather to pray during the month of Ramadan.

On September 23, Saudis celebrate Unification Day. This national holiday honors the founding of Saudi Arabia in 1932.

What are the traditional foods of Saudi Arabia?

Many Saudi foods came from the Arab lifestyle. People roaming the deserts ate foods they could carry easily, such as rice and dates. Sheep, goats, and camels provided milk and meat. Travelers from other countries brought vegetables and spices. In time, these foods were used together in dishes eaten today.

Fact!

Many people in Saudi Arabia eat a dip called hummus. Hummus is made from chickpeas. Some people spread it on sandwiches.

During special meals, families may eat together on the floor.

Many Saudi dishes today include meat, rice, vegetables, wheat, and spices. *Kebsa* is a popular dish. Saudis prepare *kebsa* by cooking rice with meat and spices in a pot. People also eat a bread called *khubz*. They eat this flat bread with meat and vegetables.

What is family life like in Saudi Arabia?

Most Saudi families are large. Aunts, uncles, and grandparents may live with the family. Families spend much time together.

Men head the household. They work and shop. Many women stay home to care for the children and cook meals. Some women attend college or work.

What are the ethnic backgrounds of people in Saudi Arabia?

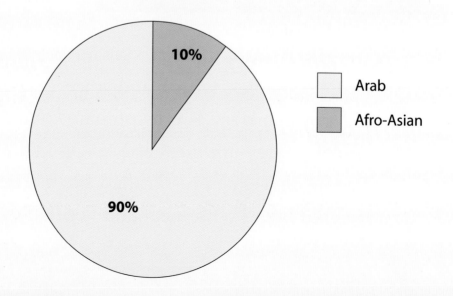

Saudi women wear black cloaks when they are out in public.

Outside of the family, women must stay very separate from men. Following Islamic law, women cover themselves with a black cloak and veil. They need to wear this outfit when they leave their home.

27

Saudi Arabia Fast Facts

Official name:

Kingdom of Saudi Arabia

Population:

25,795,938 people

Land area:

756,981 square miles
(1,960,581 square kilometers)

Capital city:

Riyadh

Average annual precipitation (Riyadh):

4 inches (10 centimeters)

Language:

Arabic

Average January temperature (Riyadh):

68 degrees Fahrenheit
(20 degrees Celsius)

Natural resources:

copper, gold, iron ore, natural gas, petroleum

Average July temperature (Riyadh):

109 degrees Fahrenheit
(43 degrees Celsius)

Religion:

Islamic   100%

Money and Flag

Money:

The Saudi riyal is Saudi Arabia's basic unit of currency. In 2004, about 3.75 Saudi riyals equaled 1 U.S. dollar. About 2.76 Saudi riyals equaled 1 Canadian dollar.

Flag:

The flag of Saudi Arabia is green, the color of Islam. It has a sentence in Arabic, "There is no God but Allah, and Muhammad is his prophet." These words are the Islamic Statement of Faith. The sword below the words shows that Saudis will fight to defend and spread Islam.

Learn to Speak Arabic

People in Saudi Arabia speak Arabic. It is Saudi Arabia's official language. Learn to speak some Arabic using the words below.

English	Arabic	Pronunciation
hello	marhaba	(MAR-hab-ah)
good-bye	ma'a s-salama	(MAH-ah sah-LAH-mah)
please	min fadlak	(MIHN FAHD-lahk)
thank you	shokran	(show-KRAHN)
yes	aywa	(EYE-wah)
no	laa	(LAH)

Glossary

adobe (uh-DOH-bee)—a building material made of clay mixed with straw and dried in the sun

calligraphy (kuh-LIG-ruh-fee)—the art of drawing or painting words

constitution (kon-stih-TOO-shuhn)—the written system of laws in a country that state the rights of people and the powers of government

Koran (kor-AHN)—the holy book of the Islamic religion

monarchy (MON-ar-kee)—a government led by a king or queen

mosque (MOSK)—a building used by Muslims for worship

Muslim (MUHZ-luhm)—a person who follows the religion of Islam; Islam is a religion whose followers believe in one god, Allah, and that Muhammad is his prophet.

nomad (NOH-mad)—a person who moves from place to place to find food and water

petroleum (puh-TROH-lee-um)—an oily liquid found below the earth's surface; it is made into gasoline.

plateau (pla-TOH)—an area of high, flat land

prophet (PROF-it)—a person who speaks or claims to speak for a god

Internet Sites

FactHound offers a safe, fun way to find Internet sites related to this book. All of the sites on FactHound have been researched by our staff.

Here's how:
1. Visit *www.facthound.com*
2. Type in this special code **0736837604** for age-appropriate sites. Or enter a search word related to this book for a more general search.
3. Click on the **Fetch It** button.

FactHound will fetch the best sites for you!

Read More

Anderson, Laurie Halse. *Saudi Arabia*. Globe-trotters Club. Minneapolis: Carolrhoda Books, 2001.

Temple, Bob. *Saudi Arabia*. Faces and Places. Chanhassen, Minn.: Child's World, 2000.

Walsh, Kieran. *Saudi Arabia*. Countries in the News. Vero Beach, Fla.: Rourke, 2004.

Index